THE LIFE
I ALWAYS WANTED

*My story of heartbreak, healing,
faith, humility and finding God*

by ANAIAH KIRK

Copyright © 2011 Anaiah Kirk
The Life I Always Wanted
by Anaiah Kirk
Printed in the United States of America
ISBN 978-0-615-45153-4

All rights reserved solely by the author. The author guarantees all content is original and does not infringe upon the legal right of any other person or work. No part of this book may be reproduced in any form without the permission of the author. All Scripture quotations in this publication are taken from the Holy Bible, New International Version®. Copyright © 1973, 1978, 1984 by International Bible Society. Used by permission of Zondervan. All rights reserved.

Design: Jeribai Tascoe, NewCreationStudio.com
Marketing: Mel Kirk, MGKvisions.com
Publishing: CreateSpace.com

For book sales or to meet the author, go to:
www.TheLifeIAlwaysWanted.com

All Scripture quotations in this publication are taken from the Holy Bible, New International Version®. Copyright © 1973, 1978, 1984 by International Bible Society. Used by permission of Zondervan. All rights reserved.

DEDICATION

I dedicate this book to my daughter Mimi and my children which are yet to be born. My hope is that you will find faith in God at a young age and never turn from Him. If you search for Him, you will find Him, and if you put Him first you won't regret it.

- Love Papa

ACKNOWLEDGMENTS

My Wife – Thank you for your support while writing this book and for your future support as I embark on finishing the sequel book. I am the luckiest guy on earth to have you. You're an amazing mother to our daughter, an awesome wife and my best friend. I love you.

My Mother - Thank you for always seeing the best in me and encouraging me in everything I do.

My Father - Thank you for not giving up on me. Your prayers are probably the reason why I am here today. Thank you for your example of faith.

Grandpa - Even though your gone, the idea of telling you that I wrote a book would probably have made you laugh hysterically. Who would have ever thought? I miss you and will always remember what you said: "Good is the Enemy of Great."

Brother and Sister: We have been through it all and we came out on top. Love you guys. Mel, thank you for business/marketing help.

Jeribai - Thank you for your design work for this book.

Kathy - Thank you for your editing work, you did an amazing job.

ENDORSEMENTS

"Anaiah's experiences are communicated in such a down to earth and personal way that all people can relate to them. The book is suprising in it's honesty... It's an ideal resrouce for church youth groups."
~ *Christian Today*

In a world where young people are always looking for something that always appears just out of their grasp, Anaiah Kirk has managed to deliver a book, a message, a life that cuts through all the fluff and glamour and reaches into the heart of the youth. In a simple yet profound way, Anaiah displays his life in complete transparency to the reader. Unafraid and unassuming, this book will find its way into many of the hearts and minds of the young people of this world by leading them down a life path that although filled with pitfalls and confusion, this life story offers hope and clarity along the journey.

And what a journey it is. The reader will feel at times like they are on a roller coaster ride of life yet it is a ride that many young people embark upon in a variety of ways. In the end, this book will deliver you safely to a place that you really wanted to be at all along and leave you with an anticipation of what is to come and how the next ride is going to be.

I would strongly recommend this book to all young people

who are searching for hope, truth, love and a real walk with the Lord.

~ Bob Wilk, Dean of the School of Ministry at
Word of Life Fellowship

Anaiah's story is an encouraging an exciting story reminding us that God both works in mysterious ways and always has a plan. After reading The Life I Always Wanted I found a deep motivation to read the Bible and spend time in prayer, something I have struggled with for many years. Like Anaiah, I too want to have a closer relationship with God, know what His will is for my life and hear him speak to me.
~ Benjamin Willemssen (age 21)

I have the distinct privilege of knowing the author for several years. This book, detailing his life story, is of a young man who seemingly had everything, only to find his life spiraling out of control. Like many of the young men I have mentored for years, he eventually "hit bottom" and turned to God out of desperation. His life story is compelling and gripping. Like me, you will relate to many of his experiences.

"The Lord had given me a second chance. He'd healed areas of my heart that were so scarred I didn't even realize they were wounded. He restored relationships and gave me the ability to trust and love again." This quote from his book is a clear summary of his life, and the compelling reason he writes his story for us to read. As you read his life story, a multitude of emotions may rise up within you. Will you, like Anaiah, find the courage to turn those emotions to God. I challenge you to read his story completely, and then follow the advice he offers.

~ *Bob Lane, International Youth Speaker & Principal at Christian Academy, Collinsville (IL)*

I really enjoyed this book; I want to read it again. It got my attention and made me want to be a better person. Before I read the book, I thought I would want to experience the lifestyle that Anaiah lived before he started to live for God, Now I can see that path does not lead to fulfillment in life.
~ *Elijah Flores, (age 15)*

This book is required reading for every young man (or woman) who has ever struggled to understand their destiny, hopes and dreams. You will discover God's love, man's love and how they fit together.
~ *John Pradenas, Youth Pastor*

TABLE OF CONTENTS

Forward		11
Introduction		13
Chp. 1	**The Life I Thought I Always Wanted**	17
Chp. 2	**The Beginning of the End**	23
Chp. 3	**Losing Everything**	35
Chp. 4	**Turning Point**	43
Chp. 5	**First Believing**	51
Chp. 6	**Meeting With God**	55
Chp. 7	**Upside Down**	57
Chp. 8	**Rock Bottom**	63
Chp. 9	**Changed**	67
Chp. 10	**Fighting For It**	73
Chp. 11	**Equipped**	77
Chp. 12	**Trials**	83
Chp. 13	**Conclusion**	87

Forward

In a culture where both loneliness and selfishness seem to rage in epidemic proportions, Anaiah's story strikes a chord of truth in providing answers to man's deepest thoughts. His story is refreshingly honest and down to earth. He dares put down his mask. It doesn't hide the egocentric and the ugly, but in the same breath it provides the beauty of grace that transforms. I would encourage every young person (and everyone else for that matter) to take up and read Anaiah's journey. You may find yourself walking with him. You may find yourself arriving at the same beautiful destination.

Pastor Dennis Ortmann.
Chapel in the Pines. Twain Harte, Ca.

Introduction

In 2003, at the age of eighteen, I thought I was on top of the world. I was about to embark on a career as a professional competitive freestyle skier, allowing me to travel the world and live an exciting lifestyle. However, in the winter of 2004, everything changed. As a result of two serious head injuries, I lost my job, and my girlfriend, and was forced to quit doing what I lived for: skiing.

At the lowest point in my life, I found something I wasn't looking for and achieved something I didn't realize I wanted: a relationship with Jesus Christ.

God began to make Himself a reality to me, which led me to let go of my old lifestyle and embrace a new one. I chose to start a relationship with God. Soon after, I had a life-changing encounter that erased all my doubts about God. I realized that knowing Him and His will for me was the life I always wanted.

This book describes the rise and fall of my skiing career and my personal life. I hope that by reading my story, you'll find parallels in your own life.

I pray that, just as I found God in my circumstances, you'll find Him too.

To aid in this voyage of discovery, I've included some Questions to Think About at the back of the book. During the story, I've inserted this — ∑ **QTA** ⊰ — in places where I would encourage you to stop and turn to the back. Read the Questions to Think About, ponder them, and jot down your thoughts either in this book or in a journal or notebook.

Doing this will help you to see this book as more than some stranger's memoir, but as a tool to help you apply the spiritual truths here to yourself and your own life.

If you'd prefer to read the story without interruption, you can wait till the end to read the Questions to Think About. Whichever way you do it, I hope you'll find this story—and the Questions to Think About—relevant and applicable, and that it will draw you closer to the God who loves you more than you can imagine.

I Thought I Had It All . . .

Chapter 1
The Life I Thought I Always Wanted

"Anaiah, are you ready?" said the announcer from the U.S. Free Skier Open.

"Yeah." I was ready but nervous as I took slow deep breaths.

"OK. Up next is The Anaiahlator from Mammoth Lakes, California. Three, two, one, go."

As I left the start gate and headed down the mountain toward the jumps, I did my best to soak in every moment. Just three years prior, I could barley ski, let alone do tricks. Now here I was, in my first major competition, the U.S. Open in Vail, Colorado, competing against some of the best freestyle skiers in the world. People who'd inspired me to ski.

I readied myself for the first jump. I had a good start, but at this level of competition, I had to do everything perfectly.

As I gained speed I heard a whistling sound as air blew through my helmet. The noise got louder and louder until I was air borne. As I flew, every sound disappeared.

My body went upside down and sideways. I saw the white snow turn into blue sky. I grabbed my skis and continued to float through the air. My body felt weightless.

My skis came back to the earth. I landed backward as though I'd never left the ground—so far so good.

I continued to ski backward toward the next jump. My speed increased. Usually I slowed down to make sure I didn't overshoot the landing, but this was the U.S. Open and I wanted to go as high and far as I could. As I shot up into the air backward, I dropped my shoulder, sending me into a sideways flip. While spinning in midair I saw the crowd on the sidelines disappear and reappear over and over.

I landed the jump backward, just as planned. Immediately I turned around to prepare myself for the biggest jump of the competition. I'd saved my best trick for last.

As I approached the jump I saw Red Bull banners waving in the wind. The crowd got louder. Two large TV screens were focused on me.

I threw myself parallel to the ground and pulled my body in tight to spin three full rotations while holding on to my skis. As I came out of my third rotation, I saw the landing come to my feet. Doing a cork 1080 wasn't easy, but this jump was huge, which gave me plenty of air time to complete the trick.

After landing, I threw my arms up in excitement. I'd completed a perfect run.

That day I ranked twenty-ninth out of more than two hundred, which qualified me for a Big Air competition the next evening. I was excited over my success, but I didn't want to just qualify; I wanted to win. I'd won most of my competitions back in California.

The next day I placed thirteenth out of 170 by completing another cork 1080. My performance caught the attention of a couple of major ski companies who offered to sponsor me. They agreed to pay for all my product and travel expenses. If they liked what they saw, both on and off the slopes, I would be offered a position on the freestyle skiing team.

That would be a dream come true. I'd travel the world, ski the best parks and powder, party, appear in films, and ski in all the major competitions. And if things didn't work out with my girlfriend, Lauren, there would be plenty of other women to meet.

Thrilled about my success, my new ski sponsors, and my potential future as a professional skier, I went back home to Mammoth Lakes, fired up to train hard and compete again. While flying over the mountains of Utah, I realized I was finally living the life I always wanted.

Or so I thought.

Little did I know, I was about to lose everything that meant the most to me.

Chapter 2
The Beginning of the End

At 5:30 one January morning, I reluctantly pulled off my warm covers, sat up, and looked out the window. The previous day's snow storm had cleared and I could see stars hovering in the sky. My one-bedroom apartment was bitterly cold, so I climbed out of bed and started the tea kettle, figuring the steam from the boiling water would bring the temperature of the apartment up three or four degrees.

While the water was boiling, I took a shower, leaving the bathroom door open so the room temperature could raise a bit more. I could've turned on the heater, but I was a cheapskate. Besides, I didn't care about warmth. This winter was all about taking another step toward fulfilling my dream of freestyle skiing professionally.

When I got out of the shower, I ate breakfast and did my homework in psychology, criminal justice, and English. I finished around eight, ready to head up to the mountain for another day of skiing.

I was one of the first in line for the gondola. As I rode up, I noticed that the terrain park, a ski run full of jumps, was groomed and ready to open. This was rare. Usually after the mountain got snow, it took at least half a day to open.

Although excited about the twelve new inches of powder, I was even more thrilled about practicing the bio 900 I'd recently learned. The trick involved two and a half rotations while facing parallel to the ground.

When the gondola reached the halfway station, I hopped out, clipped on my skis, and took off for the terrain park, where I did my usual routine. I slid some rails which are hand rails placed in the snow for skiers and snowboarders to slide across, performed a 360 (single spin) off two of the smaller jumps, and did a rodeo (which involves a sideways flip with one and a half spins) off a medium jump (around fifty-five feet).

At the end of the terrain park was the "money booster," a jump approximately seventy feet long. I could usually figure out everything about a jump just by looking at it from a distance, but when there was new snow, I resorted to testing the jumps. In previous practice sessions, the first time I went off the money booster, I usually took it straight, with no spins, or at the most a simple 360. This allowed me to see how much speed I had and whether I needed more or less next time around. It also let me get a feel for how steep the takeoff was, how much time I'd have in the air, how hard or soft the landing was, the wind effects, and so on.

That day, for some reason, the thought of testing the jump never crossed my mind. I guess I was too preoccupied with the idea of trying the trick I had learned just a few days before.

At the top of the money booster, I checked my helmet strap, secured my goggles, and pointed my skis toward the jump. Shortly after I started the run, I realized I had a little too much speed going, so I gave two check turns, which slowed me down. As I neared the jump, I visualized what my body positioning would be from takeoff to landing.

The last foot of the jump had a hump in it, which caused me to go an extra seven feet or so higher than I expected. It was like hitting a speed bump in a parking lot going thirty-five mph. The moment I went airborne, I knew I was going too high and too fast.

As I finished my first rotation, I saw the landing go past my feet. All I could do was uncork myself and hope to absorb most of the impact with my legs.

I overshot the landing by thirty feet. When my skis touched the snow, my head whipped backward, knocking me unconscious.

The memories of what happened after I woke up are blurred. I remember picking up my skis and getting back on the chair lift, then standing at the top of the run being examined by a ski patroller, with all my friends standing around me. I have no recollection of riding up the lift. It's a miracle I didn't fall off.

A friend skied down with me to the parking lot, where another friend picked me up and took me home. I had a splitting headache and almost threw up three times.

The next morning I awoke feeling worse. The right side of my brain was pounding, my memory was full of holes, and the nausea lingered. I'd had concussions before: one while playing soccer, two caused by hockey, and the other two from skiing. But this one felt different.

I knew some serious damage had been done.

I called the doctor's office and spoke to a physician over the phone. I told him about the crash and how I felt. He asked if I had any previous head injuries, which I reluctantly confessed to.

He was quiet for quite some time. Then he told me about the famous boxer Mohammed Ali, whose multiple head injuries led to his contracting Alzheimer's disease. "Do you remember quarterback Steve Young?" he asked.

"Of course I do," I said.

"Do you know why he had to retire from football?"

"No."

"He had a history of concussions. Each one increased the chance that he would have major brain damage, perhaps even go into a coma."

"What are you saying? I should never ski again?"

"I didn't say you can't ski anymore. But I don't recommend it for at least a month."

"A month!" The biggest competitions were coming up in about six weeks. "Can't I just wear a better helmet?"

"It's your call, kid. I'm just giving you my advice. Take it or leave it."

With great reluctance, I decided I would not ski for a month, or at least until I felt 100 percent.

Two days later, after I got out of work, I called my friend Adam. "What's going on tonight?"

"A bunch of us are going to a party near the resort at Victor's house. You've gotta go. There's gonna be a ton of girls."

My girlfriend Lauren and I had decided to take a "dating break" a few weeks earlier. We were constantly arguing, and when I found out she was hanging out with another guy, I called it quits for the time being, even though I loved her.

I told Adam to meet me at the Chevron station so I could follow him to the party. When we got together, Adam told me some skinheads were going to be there.

"Why should I care?" I asked.

"Just be careful. I hear those guys are trouble."

The first couple of hours at the party were a blast. I met lots of girls and tried to get as many phone numbers as possible. Lauren was there with her new guy friend. She seemed to notice how well I was doing with the ladies, and I enjoyed making her squirm.

One girl I met that night was Sarah. She was extremely attractive. And she was into me. I led her into the middle of the party, where everybody, including Lauren, could see the two of us together.

When the night got late, I decided to go home. As I was walking across the living room, toward the stairs that led down to the door, I saw a mutual friend of Lauren's and mine. Rebecca, who was sitting on a couch, caught me and started asking questions about whether Lauren and I would ever get back together. I didn't like her interrogation. So when Adam pulled me away, I was grateful for the reprieve.

He told me the skinheads had been staring at me all night, and he was afraid something bad might happen if I didn't leave soon.

"That's crazy," I said. To prove that I wasn't intimidated, I returned to the couch and resumed my conversation with Rebecca. As soon as Adam was out of sight, I ended the conversation, stood, and said good-bye.

I reached down to give Rebecca a hug, and as I let go, one of the skinheads grabbed me and slammed my head against the wall. Two guys started punching me in the head. I blanked out for a few seconds, then found myself at the bottom of the stairs. One of the skinheads yelled, "I'm going to kill you," adding a curse for effect.

In a daze, I got up as quickly as I could, ran out the door, and fled down the street. Within a few feet, I slipped on an icy section and fell, hitting my head again. I got to my feet and jumped into a ditch on the side of the road. I lay there for a few minutes, trying to figure out what had happened.

Back at the house, I heard everybody screaming at the skinheads. "Why did you do that? Do you even know who that guy is? What did he ever do to you?"

Afraid these guys might come out and find me, I called the police on my cell phone. I stayed in the ditch, shivering, until they arrived. As soon as they went into the house, I crawled out and headed toward home.

My phone rang. Caller ID told me it was Lauren. She called about twenty times. I didn't answer until I was a safe distance from the house.

"Are you okay?"

"No, I'm not okay. I got my head beat on!"

"Where are you? I need to see you."

"When you leave the house, turn left and then walk down the street about half a mile. And don't tell anybody." I didn't want anyone but her to see me.

As I sat on the curb waiting for her, my thoughts raced. Was I going to be able to ski in a month? Would I be able to ski at all this season? I also thought about how nice it was to hear Lauren sound so concerned about me. Perhaps this incident would bring us back together. Maybe she would appreciate me more.

I heard footsteps running toward me. I lifted my head, painful though that was. To my deep disappointment, Lauren was not alone. She'd brought her new boyfriend, Brodie, with her.

Confused and upset, I got up and started to walk away. She grabbed me by the arm. "Let me see your head."

I leaned over.

"You're bleeding."

"Why should you care?"

My head was in splitting pain, my vision blurry, and my speech slurred.

While Lauren examined me, I glared at Brodie, who stood beside me, trying to hold me up. "Do you really love her?" I was convinced there was only one reason he was with her.

He looked at her, then at me. "Don't worry about that, bud. Let's just take care of you."

"Do you love her?" I yelled.

Before he could answer, two friends came up and offered to take me to their friend's house. I accepted their invitation, eager to get away from the two lovebirds. Unfortunately, they followed.

Once we got to the house, people surrounded me, including Rebecca. The police arrived, and they took my statement as well as statements from my friends who'd witnessed the attack. The cops recommend I take an ambulance to the hospital to get checked out, but I declined, afraid the medical bills would cost too much.

After the police left, I asked Rebecca if she knew why I was jumped. She told me she heard that the girl I was flirting with, Sarah, was an ex-girlfriend of one of the guys who beat me up. Four of the skinheads who were at the party had warrants out for their arrest. Apparently Sarah had slept with all four of them.

"But she was talking to other guys besides me. Why didn't they get hit?"

"I don't know. Maybe because you were with her the longest and you got her phone number. But don't worry; they're going to get what they deserve."

"What do you mean?"

"Some of my friends went to their house and broke their windows, smashed their TV, and slit their car tires." She started to tell me the names of her friends who had destroyed all that stuff, but I stopped her.

If the police found out about the vandalism, they would point the finger at me, and I wanted nothing to do with somebody else's retaliatory actions.

I ached to go home and try to sleep, but Lauren insisted that it would be best if I stayed with her for the night. I agreed, hoping we would be able to talk about the possibility of getting back together.

As soon as we arrived at her place, she took me up to her room and laid me on her bed. Within seconds I fell asleep.

I woke up to a bright light. For a second, I thought I'd died and gone to heaven, but when I regained consciousness, I realized that someone was shining a flashlight in my eyes. Apparently, my girlfriend had been trying to wake me up for ten minutes.

Once I was awake, she took me to her father, a firefighter.

We got to her dad's house around three in the morning. He checked my pupils and found out they were not dilating. He insisted I go to the hospital. Tired and in pain, I reluctantly went.

As I sat in the waiting room, I found it hard to stay awake. I asked Lauren to keep talking to me so I wouldn't fall asleep. For a few minutes, I felt as though we were back together. She even held my hand and put her head on my shoulder.

After examining me, the doctor told me I needed an MRI. He was worried there might be bleeding in my head. That scared me. Not only was my ski season at risk, but now I was being told my life may be in danger.

While I was in the MRI machine, my body shook uncontrollably. The trembling became so bad, the doctor had to restart the test twice.

After reviewing my MRI, the doctor found no signs of bleeding; however, he was convinced that this concussion was a warning for me to stop skiing for the remainder of the season.

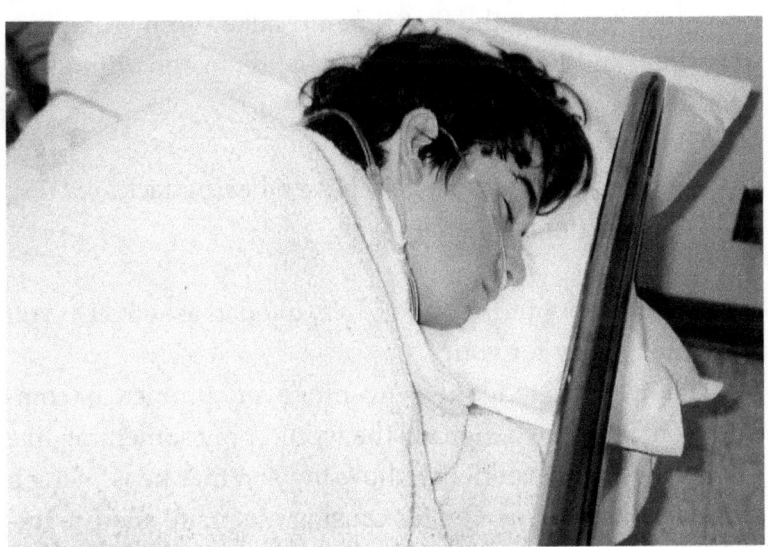

Once I got home, I collapsed. I hadn't slept in twenty-four hours, my head was spinning, and Lauren had announced on the ride back from the hospital that she was going snowboarding the next day with Brodie.

I thought about calling my dad. I wondered if he would be concerned, or if he'd say his usual, "Well, that's what you deserve for not putting the Lord first." I knew that when everybody back home found out I'd stopped skiing, they'd think I was a screw-up.

After a warm bath, I put on my pajamas and lay in bed, still thinking about calling my father. I finally decided to just get it over with.

"Hi, Dad."

"Why are you calling?"

"Something happened that I thought you should know about." I gave him a five-minute explanation.

"Well, that's what happens when you hang out at parties." I kept my mouth shut, afraid I would say something I'd regret. This was the first time I'd talked to my dad in a long time, and I wanted the conversation to end with us on good terms.

"Does your mother know?"

"Not yet. I was afraid she'd have a heart attack."

"You'd better call her anyway."

"I will."

As I was about to say good-bye, my dad asked, "Do you want me to pray for you?"

That was his standard answer for every problem or complication. I hesitated, figuring he would pray something like "Lord, may this experience show my son that he is living a sinful life" or "Thank You for causing him pain, and use this to bring him home where he belongs." But for some reason I said yes.

To my surprise, Dad gave a quick, simple prayer that my head would be healed.

"Thanks, Dad. I'll talk to you later."

Relieved that the conversation was over, I hung up the phone.

Feeling a little better, I decided to call my mom. If she found out about my injury from anyone else, she would be really upset.

"Hi, Mom."

"Hello, Anaiah. What's going on?"

"I need you to sit down. I have something to tell you."

"Oh, my God. What happened? Are you okay? Are you bleeding? Did you hit your head again?"

"Relax, Mom. I'm okay. But yes, I did hit my head again."

After I explained what happened, she went into mother freak-out mode. "Where are those kids? I'm going to kill them! Are the cops out looking for them?"

"Calm down, Mom. They'll get caught sooner or later." After talking for a short time we ended the conversation with I-love-yous.

The following Monday I went back to college. My head was hurting and I had trouble concentrating. By the end of each class I had forgotten most of the information we'd covered. To make matters worse, my speech slurred whenever I spoke.

That night my mother called to see how I was doing. I told her about my symptoms.

"I'm calling your aunt right now and taking you to Stanford to get checked out by a neurologist." My aunt worked in the library at Stanford University near San Francisco, and she knew several doctors there. I knew I needed to see a specialist. I agreed to let her make the call.

The next day, I went to work after school as usual. I was a busboy at one of the finest restaurants in Mammoth. As I was setting a table, I forgot where the plates and silverware went. No matter how long I stared at the table, it didn't come to me. I had been working there for months, but I felt like it was my first day.

I went outside to get some fresh air and to think. If I couldn't remember anything, there wasn't much point in my going to school or work. Maybe I should move back in with my mom, recover, save up some money, and come back next season. I also wondered if I should try to make things work with Lauren.

As I stood outside in the freezing wind, staring at the mountains, I could not believe how fast everything around me had changed. Where would I go from here?

Chapter 3
Losing Everything

That weekend, I had an appointment at Stanford Medical. If the doctor there thought I should go home to recover, I would consider it. If he thought I would be okay in a few weeks, I'd go back to Mammoth.

On the way to Stanford, I stopped by my dad's place to see my brother. Mel gave me a hug and asked how I was doing.

"Things could be better. Is Dad here?" I knew it would be easier for us to talk if he wasn't around.

"Yeah, he's upstairs."

Just then my dad came down the steps. "Hello, Anaiah."

"Hi, Dad." I didn't feel like talking to him, but I was happy to see his face. For some strange reason, I gave him a hug. "It's good to see you."

After talking for a little while, I left and went to my mother's house.

The next day Mom and I drove to San Francisco. When we arrived at my grandmother's, she had prepared one of her usual to-die-for Italian dinners. I was hungry, but I couldn't eat because my two aunts asked question after question about what had happened to me. I finally told them I was tired and went to take a nap.

The next day I saw the family doctor. He told me the same thing the doctor at the Mammoth hospital said. "I don't think you should ski anymore this year." The guy was in his seventies and seemed overly cautious.

On Monday I went to Stanford Medical Center, where I was examined by one of the country's top neurologists. He performed a few memorization tests. In one, he would tell me a word, such as toy, and ask me to say the word three times. Then he asked questions about where I lived and my dog's name. This continued for fifteen to twenty seconds. Then he asked me to restate the word I'd said three times. At first I laughed. But when I realized I couldn't remember a simple word like toy, I became frustrated.

After a few more tests, the doctor told me my memory loss and slurred speech were due to all my head injuries.

"Are you saying I should stop skiing for a while?"

"I can't make you do anything. But if you hit your head again in the next six to nine months, you have a seventy-five percent chance of going into a coma."

I wondered what I was going to do. My whole life was wrapped up in skiing. I'd trained hard and made many choices based on my focus on skiing. This was the most important year for me if I was going to make skiing my profession. What would my sponsors say?

On the drive back to my grandmother's house, I decided to call off my skiing for the remainder of the season. Later that day I e-mailed my manager and told him what the doctor had said. I assured him that I would be back to skiing the following season.

In his e-mail response, he said he was sorry about what happened and wished there was something he could do. Then he said that the sponsor contract I was supposed to sign within a few months was now out of the question.

My dream was shattered. I sat at my grandmother's computer, trying not to cry.

I had to get out of the house, but my mom had driven me there and was not coming back until the next day. I decided to take my aunt's dog for a walk. When I got to the top of the street, I came to an overlook of the San Carlos hills. I could see the entire Bay Area, including San Francisco. I felt like I was in one of those movies where the car pulls up to the make-out point overlooking the city with his girlfriend. Only I was alone.

I sat on a fire hydrant on the side of the road. As I pulled off my sweatshirt, my cell phone fell to the ground and opened. When I picked it up, I saw a name I hadn't seen in over a year: Aimee.

I'd known Aimee since fourth grade. I had a crush on her on and off since the seventh grade. Her big hazel eyes could look right into me. With just one glance, she made me feel like I was the most rotten person on earth. But other times she gazed at me and made me feel warm and good. The whole time I'd known Aimee, she was a strong Christian.

Every conversation we had in high school was uncomfortable. Whenever we talked to each other, our voices cracked, our eyes refused to meet, and our bodies sent out weird vibes. We both knew we liked each other. But we could never get over our nervousness.

I hadn't talked to her since I left for college two years

earlier. I had no idea why her name had popped up on my cell-phone screen. Wondering how she was doing, I called her.

"This is Aimee. Please leave your name and number after the beep."

"Hi, Aimee, it's Anaiah. I'm here at Stanford. I was just thinking about you and wanted to give you a call, see how you're doing. Call me back if you want. Talk to you later. Bye."

I felt both relieved and disappointed that she hadn't answered.

The next day Mom picked me up from my grandmother's house and we headed back to her place.

That night I went to Dad's house to tell him what the doctor at Stanford said. He said he was sorry but did not seem concerned about my medical well being. I felt he was more concerned about my spiritual well being. My brother on the other hand, seemed to show me more pity.

After dinner I went back to Mom's. When I went up to my room, I saw I had a missed a phone call from a friend in Mammoth. I called him back. He asked how I was doing.

After I explained what the Stanford doctor had said, he told me he was sorry. He also said he knew something he thought I ought to hear.

"What is it?" I asked.

"Something's up with Lauren. I drove by her house the other day and saw a guy walk into her house."

"So what? She can hang out with other guys."

"Yeah, I know. But I drove by early the next morning and saw him walking away from her house."

"You mean he spent the night there?"

"Look, Anaiah, I don't want to get involved, so don't tell her I told you, okay?"

I hung up the phone and started to panic. Was Lauren sleeping with this guy? Should I go to Mammoth and confront her? Or should I pretend that my friend never told me?

I had to know the truth. My heart pounding, I called her.

"Hello?"

"Hi, it's me." I tried to keep my voice calm. If she suspected I was up to something, she would hang up.

"I'm watching a movie with friends," she whispered.

"Do you think you could go someplace where you could talk?"

"Okay."

I heard a guy ask who was on the phone. She whispered, "It's him."

Several moments later, she spoke to me again. "Why did you call me?"

I told her what the Stanford doctors said.

"What are you going to do?" She sounded concerned.

"That depends. I want to ask you a question and I need an honest answer."

"Okay."

"Do you love me?"

After a few seconds of silence, she said, "Anaiah, I love you and always will."

"Do you mean that?" I had a lot resting on her answer.

"Yes, I do."

"Do you want us to be together again?"

"Definitely."

"Then why are you hanging out with this other guy?"

"He's just a friend."

I wanted to ask if she'd spent the night with this friend, but was afraid to ask. "Okay. I'll call you later tonight."

I wanted to believe she was telling the truth. But if she really loved me, she wouldn't be hanging out with other guys. Especially not overnight.

I decided to leave for Mammoth right away. When I told my dad, we argued. I yelled, packed my stuff, and headed out about 11:30 p.m.

The drive to Mammoth usually took anywhere from four and a half to six hours, but that night I made it home in three. Since my stereo had recently been stolen from my '91 Toyota Tercel, all I could hear was the constant grinding of studded tires on the road. All I could think about was what Lauren may be doing with this guy.

I drove into town around 2:30 a.m. A light snow came down. No cars were on the road. The place was dead silent. When I got to Lauren's street, I turned off my lights. I parked three houses away so that if they were in the living room, they wouldn't see me.

As I approached the driveway, the motion-sensor light came on and I saw tire tracks of a car that had come and gone. There were two sets of footprints. I figured one was Lauren's, but who'd made the others? I took a deep breath and headed up the porch stairs.

I entered through the side door, which was always unlocked. The house was dark and quiet, but warm. I took a deep breath and headed toward the bedroom.

When I opened the door I heard the bed sheets shuffle. I turned on the light. As my eyes focused, I saw what I had dreaded: the two of them in bed together.

"Oh, no," she moaned when she realized it was me. "This

can't be happening." She pushed Brodie out of the bed. He landed with a thump, then curled up on the floor in a daze.

Lauren started getting dressed. I screamed and swore at her. Determined not to do something I'd regret, I bolted down the hall toward the front door.

Lauren grabbed my arm. I couldn't even look at her, much less say anything, so I yanked out of her grasp and stormed outside.

"Anaiah, wait," she yelled, but I didn't.

She caught up with me at the car. "It's not what you think."

"You were in bed with another guy. What else is there to think?"

"Please, we need to talk."

I got in the driver's seat, but before I could take off, she climbed into the passenger seat. "We didn't have sex. Brodie just had too much to drink and needed a place to stay for the night."

I wanted to believe her. I debated whether I should try to get her back or end our relationship. For some crazy reason I tried to convince her to come back to me.

We talked for three hours. As the sun began to rise, she said, "Brodie's inside waiting for me. I need to go talk to him."

I told her I'd be back in five hours, after she'd gotten some sleep. But instead of leaving, I sat in my car, freezing.

I wondered what I would do if Lauren left me for this guy. For the first time in my life, I had thoughts of suicide. I was losing everything: skiing, my girlfriend, school, work. The choices I'd made over the past two years had led me to a sudden dead end, with no hope in sight.

When Lauren came back outside, we drove a few miles out of town to an old road where we used to walk her dog. For three hours we talked about life, where we had come from, where we were, and what was to come of us. I tried desperately to convince her that I loved her and that we needed to start over. But nothing I said seemed to make any difference.

She kept saying vague things like "I love you and I know I will be with you, just not now" and "I need to see other people so I can have stronger feelings for you." I told her I understood, but I didn't.

When I got home, I put my head down on the kitchen counter and cried.

Σ **QTA** ⋛

Chapter 4
Turning Point

While I sat in the kitchen, crying over Lauren and everything that had occurred over the last week, I noticed a book on the counter. It was a Bible. I wondered how it got there.

"Okay, Lord, what is it You want from me?" I decided to open it, and if God didn't speak to me with what I read, I would never touch a Bible again.

I randomly opened it and it ended up in Hosea. I read the entire book. As I did, I felt like I was reading a note God had written directly to me.

The book of Hosea records how the Israelites turned their backs on God by ignoring Him and choosing to do things that were sins in God's eyes. In Hosea 1:2, the Lord told Hosea, "Go, take to yourself an adulterous wife and children of unfaithfulness, because the land is guilty of the vilest adultery in departing from the Lord." So he married a prostitute named Gomer, and she bore him a son.

When I read this, I felt as though I were looking into a mirror. I realized I was being like Israel. I was behaving like a rebellious kid, and my choices had driven me away from the Lord. I was acting just like Hosea's wife, continuously cheating on God by choosing everything but Him.

To fully understand the seriousness of what the Lord was saying to me, I looked up the word adultery which is a voluntary sexual intercourse between a married man and someone other than his wife or between a married woman and someone other than her husband.

I knew the Lord was telling me I was behaving like a prostitute, giving my love to the cares of this world and not to Him. According to Exodus 20:5, God is a jealous God.

I also realized that the Lord was answering my question about whether or not I should get back with Lauren. She was in no way a prostitute; in fact, I was the prostitute. But my love was for this girl, this world, and my will, not for God.

When I woke up the next day, I felt a glimmer of hope. Although I was in the middle of losing everything I felt was important in my life, a seed of faith started growing in me. I asked the Lord to speak to me again, and then opened the Bible. This time it fell open to Luke chapter 15.

Luke 15:7 jumped out at me. It said, "There will be more rejoicing in heaven over one sinner who repents than over ninety-nine righteous persons who do not need to repent."

I wondered what the Lord wanted me to repent of.

I continued reading. I soon came to the parable known as the prodigal son. Jesus said:

There was a man who had two sons. The younger one said to his father, "Father, give me my share of the estate." So he divided his property between them. Not long after that, the younger son got together all he had, set off for a distant country and there squandered his wealth in wild living. After he had spent everything, there was a severe famine in that whole country, and he began to be in need. So he went and hired himself out to a citizen of that country, who sent him to his fields to feed pigs. He longed to fill his stomach with the pods that the pigs were eating, but no one gave him anything.

When he came to his senses, he said, "How many of my father's hired men have food to spare, and here I am starving to death! I will set out and go back to my father and say to him: Father, I have sinned against heaven and against you. I am no longer worthy to be called your son; make me like one of your hired men." So he got up and went to his father.

But while he was still a long way off, his father saw him and was filled with compassion for him; he ran to his son, threw his arms around him and kissed him.

The son said to him, "Father, I have sinned against heaven and against you. I am no longer worthy to be called your son."

But the father said to his servants, "Quick! Bring the best robe and put it on him. Put a ring on his finger and sandals on his feet. Bring the fattened calf and kill it. Let's have a feast and celebrate. For this son of mine was dead and is alive again; he was lost and is found." So they began to celebrate.

Meanwhile, the older son was in the field. When he came near the house, he heard music and dancing. So he called one of the servants and asked him what was going on.

"Your brother has come," he replied, "and your father has killed the fattened calf because he has him back safe and sound."

The older brother became angry and refused to go in. So his father went out and pleaded with him. But he answered his father, "Look! All these years I've been slaving for you and never disobeyed your orders. Yet you never gave me even a young goat so I could celebrate with my friends. But when this son of yours who has squandered your property with prostitutes comes home, you kill the fattened calf for him!"

"My son," the father said, "you are always with me, and everything I have is yours. But we had to celebrate and be glad, because this brother of yours was dead and is alive again; he was lost and is found."

As I read this parable I got teary eyed. I knew the Lord was telling me to go home. But I did not want to go.

I wondered if it was merely coincidence that I fell upon those particular Scriptures or if the Lord was truly speaking to me.

Σ QTA Ƹ

I knew the Lord was calling me to go back home and start to get to know Him better. But going home would mean a totally different lifestyle for me, and that was an uncomfortable thought. So I looked for escape routes. I told myself I didn't need to go back home to change the way I was living. I could start a relationship with God right there in Mammoth. I would begin by attending a local church.

The churches I'd been to in the area were all nice. The people were friendly. The music was good and the messages were great. But there were a few things I hadn't been able to find.

I never left the building excited or convicted. And every sermon carried the same message: worship God, love other people, tithe, and participate in water baptism. Not that those messages aren't extremely important. Jesus stated in Mathew 22:37–40:

"Love the Lord your God with all your heart and with all your soul and with all your mind. This is the first and greatest commandment. And the second is like it: Love your neighbor as yourself. All the Law and the Prophets hang on these two commandments."

This message should indeed be taken to heart every day. However, there is more to the Bible than the simple message of love and giving the church money.

When I was growing up, I heard a preacher say that there were going to be people who would do greater works than Jesus did, and they would set up God's kingdom here on earth in preparation for the Lord's return.

At the age of 7, it sounded like a fairy tale. But now, in the midst of all my troubles, the Lord was beginning to reveal Himself to me and I was starting to believe Him. Perhaps those things I'd heard growing up were true. After all, they came from the same Book that had just spoken directly to me three days in a row!

The next day I woke up early and went to church in Lake Crowley, about ten minutes down the road from Mammoth. While driving, I prayed out loud.

"Okay, God, You have my attention. I'm guessing You want me to go home, but I don't know how. If You really want me to do that, You're going to have to provide a way."

I came to the conclusion that the worst part about moving back home would be that I wouldn't have a good job. In Mammoth I worked at an awesome restaurant. The food was fantastic, my boss treated me like a son, and I earned good money. I said to God, "Couldn't I stay here until the winter is over? That way I can save up money for a newer car."

Just then my phone rang. The caller was my aunt.

"Anaiah," she said, "I don't want you living in Mammoth anymore. If you come home, I'll give you the car that's been sitting in my garage."

I told her I'd call her back and let her know.

When I got off the phone I started laughing. "I should have asked for a million dollars, God. Do you think I can switch?"

I immediately turned my car around and headed back to Mammoth to start packing my stuff. I was going home.

Σ QTA Ƹ

On Monday, when I opened the door to my mother's house, she hugged me like I was a child. "Mom, get off me, I'm fine."

My grandmother and aunts were also excited I had moved home to recover. However, tension remained between my father and me. I felt like a failure for not continuing my skiing, especially when I was surrounded by my successful father who was a world renowned engineer and my brother who was on the fast track to a successful business and marketing career.

The following Wednesday night I attended church. It was the same church I was raised in, and was the same church my father and brother still devoutly attended. I drove into the parking lot with mixed emotions. I was excited about seeing everybody again, but I also felt embarrassed. Many people here thought I was going to become a professional skier, and there I was, back at square one.

As I stepped into the foyer, I received numerous greetings and hugs. As much as I appreciated everyone's love, I was annoyed at all the attention. I wanted to be left alone. I still hadn't decided whether I would move back to Mammoth once my head injuries healed.

I walked into the sanctuary hoping to feel something spiritual, but I felt absolutely nothing. I just sat in the back row and listened to the music.

After the worship time, a man stood at the pulpit and preached a message about the prodigal son. Everything he said confirmed the decision I'd made to come home. I knew the Lord had spoken to me through His Word, through my aunt, and through the preacher.

I was definitely where the Lord wanted me. But I still wasn't sure why the Lord had brought me back.

Σ **QTA** ⊰

Chapter 5
First Believing

Living at home brought back floods of memories I hadn't thought about in years. Every room of the house contained something that made me recall an incident from my past. The photographs all reminded me of someone who'd played an important role in my childhood and youth.

Thinking that perhaps God had brought me back here, at least in part, to consider how He had orchestrated events in my life to lead me up to this moment, I spent a great deal of time sitting in my room, wandering through the house when no one else was home, and taking long drives around town, stopping whenever a particular sight, sound, or smell jogged a powerful memory.

The living room held the most pictures, so I lingered in there quite a bit, gazing at photos of myself, my parents, my older brother, Mel, and my younger sister, Shelami.

I'd grown up in a Christian family, so God was always a part of my life. But I neglected the opportunity to develop a deep foundational faith and a personal relationship with God. All I knew was that Christians got together several times a week to worship, learn, study, and love, and that in general, most church-going people lived better lives than those who didn't. Or so I thought.

As a young child I loved Sunday mornings, when my parents would drop me off at junior church. I played games with my friends, watched Christian movies, and listened to lessons about the Bible.

One of my favorite Scripture characters was Daniel. I wondered how somebody could be thrown into a den of lions for worshipping God and not be scared. My teacher told me Daniel's faith gave him that confidence. "What's faith?" I asked. The term was explained to me as "believing in someone or something with assurance."

I had no problem with that. I accepted lots of things by faith. I believed my mom was my mom, my friends were my friends, gravity pulled things down, and God sent His Son, Jesus, to save my life. Faith was as natural as breathing . . . back then.

When I was five years old, the Sunday school teacher brought up the subject of demons, which I understood to be angels for Satan. In all the pictures I'd seen of angels, they looked nice and friendly. So that night I told my mom I wanted to see a picture of a demon. She told me I didn't want to see one. But after I begged and begged, she told me to pray about it. That night I asked God if He would let me see a demon.

While I was asleep, I heard a knocking noise followed by a whispering sound, like a breeze of air. When I awoke, I knew there was something evil in my house.

I looked past my open bedroom door to the living room. There I saw a circular blood-red cloud hovering about three feet above the ground. I threw my sheets over my head, terrified. Seconds later I heard a tapping sound. I pulled down my sheets and fixed my eyes on the red cloud. It made a few circles, then slowly crept toward my room.

I jumped out of my bed and into my brother's bed, which was right above mine. I slammed the sheets over my head.

Seconds later I heard the same tapping. I poked my head between the side posts of the bed. The cloud came into my room and circled five feet away from where I was lying. I felt certain I was going to be killed by this demon, which Satan had sent to destroy me.

I screamed. Within seconds my father ran in and grabbed me. He picked me up and carried me to his bed, where I should have felt protected. But I was certain that nothing on earth could save me.

A minute or two later, I heard the tapping noise again. I opened my eyes and saw the demon come out of my room, float down the hall into the living room, and disappear.

After that night I was convinced of the existence of a spiritual world that included good and bad, righteous and demonic, God and Satan.

But that knowledge didn't really affect my day-to-day life.

Σ **QTA** Ƹ

Chapter 6
Meeting with God

Along with all the pictures of relatives in the living room, I found a few photos of my best friends from childhood. We did everything together: built forts, fished, hunted with BB guns, skied, sledded, and built skateboard parks in our driveways. The photos reminded me of days before all of us went through life's discouragements and the crisis of our faith.

A wooden cabinet with glass doors sat in one corner of the living room, proudly displaying all my sports trophies. From a young age I was involved in almost every sport imaginable, but hockey, soccer, and baseball were my favorites.

Every summer I went to church camp at Old Oak Ranch, a half-hour drive from where I lived. There my childhood faith grew and I began to understand how great God's love is, and how this love draws people to love Him and love each other.

When I was thirteen years old, I approached a small chapel at the edge of the forest surrounding Old Oak Ranch. As I neared the building, I heard the muffled sounds of men, women, and kids praying. As I came closer, the noise increased, along with a powerful feeling of awe and wonder.

I felt as though a warm blanket was covering me.

The closer I got to the chapel, the more this emotion intensified, to the point that I began to cry. By the time I entered the front doors, I had tears running down my cheeks. I thought, I don't know what this is, but I love it!

Every night that week the same thing happened, and the feeling got stronger and stronger. By the end of the week the sensation was so intense I could barely walk. I never questioned what the feeling was; I knew it was God's love. And I never wanted it to go away.

Looking back on that experience, I wanted more than anything to have that kind of relationship with God and to meet with Him daily. But how? What could I do to get back to that place of simple love, faith, and trust?

Σ **QTA** Ƹ

Chapter 7
Upside Down

On the wall between two living room windows hung a picture of my family when we were together for the last time. I was fourteen and my life was perfect. I had my family, health, friends, sports, and a solid faith in God. That was before my life was flipped upside down.

Growing up, I knew my father and mother had their ups and downs, just like any married couple. But in the fall of 1998 I came home from a Wednesday night church service and went upstairs to my room. I heard my parents arguing. This was the last night my mother and father slept under the same roof.

The next morning my mom left the house, and for the first time in my life I saw my dad cry.

At first I hoped the split would be temporary. But as weeks turned into months and months turned into seasons, I knew their marriage was over.

Still, I felt compelled to try to do something to fix it. I became a mediator between my mother and father. But as I tried to mediate between them, I learned about things they'd done to each other. My mother blamed my father for neglecting her by spending most of his time at church and work. She even blamed him for treating the pastor as if she were a god, doing whatever she asked him to do. My father never spoke harshly about my mother, but I could tell he was disappointed in her lack of faith toward God and the church.

Also during this time, I learned that my mother had feelings for another man while married to my father.

The more I learned about my parents' relationship and their struggles, the more I questioned the beliefs that had been instilled in me, such as true love and faith in relationships. I also began to struggle with the idea of church. If God created the church to uplift people and help heal them, why did my church break my family apart?

Before long, I began to see a new reality. Love was not what I thought it should be. My family was no longer a family. Church wasn't good for a person; it now

seemed like a structured dictatorship. And as for God . . . why would a loving God allow so much hurt? Was there even a God?

To make matters worse, the same time that my parents split up, some close friends of mine left the church on bad terms. I'd grown up with these people, and all of a sudden, they were gone.

More people left the church, and I wondered why. Perhaps they were finding out the same information I had discovered. I sought out the folks who'd left to find out why. I thought that if I could learn why they abandoned the church, maybe I could figure out why my mom had left us.

I expected these people to have some deep theological reasons for leaving the church. Instead I found that the church members simply weren't getting along with one another.

It felt like high school with all the stupid cliques.

I continued to question, and I kept receiving the same responses.

"They're wrong."

"They're lying."

"They did this. They did that."

At the Christian school I attended, my classmates started expressing negative attitudes about my church. The kids whose parents had left the church turned against me.

I wanted to be friends with everybody. But they didn't feel the same way.

I hoped the tension would calm down eventually. But day after day, I received nasty looks, rude remarks, and disgusted smirks from people who used to go to church with me.

I gradually lost my belief that God really cared. As my faith dwindled, I struggled more in school. I also began to believe that my parents' divorce was a result of their disagreement on how to raise me, making me ultimately responsible for the break-up. Tears flowed so much for so long, my heart finally dried up. My heart callused over and grew bitter.

At this point in my life, I struggled with the Christian faith. I'd grown up learning about loving your neighbor and even your enemy. In church I heard people talk about esteeming the other person above yourself and laying your life down for others. I heard so many good things, but I saw the opposite happening all around me. I felt those who called themselves Christians were hypocrites.

Now, as an adult, I have learned that if you're going to preach a belief, you must be willing to live that belief. Words without actions are not only meaningless, but can cause harm.

I found one of my favorite photos on top of the china cabinet in the dining room. It showed my dad, brother and sister, and me in Lake Tahoe the winter I was fifteen. On that trip, we watched skiers on the slopes doing flips and spins on snowboard jumps. I had no idea skiers could do those kinds of tricks. I was immediately drawn to the sport. That weekend I went home and bought twin-tip skies and a season pass at a local ski resort.

For me, skiing was the perfect sport. I didn't have to rely on anybody but myself to excel. I could enjoy the beauty of the mountains without any interruption of school or people. Most important, skiing allowed me to get away from home and forget about the troubles in my life.

Σ **QTA** Ƹ

Chapter 8
Rock Bottom

After gazing at the pictures on the wall, I opened a photo album under the music stand. It was covered with dust. I opened the album and saw a picture of my first car, which I got when I was sixteen. It was a 1987 gold, two-door Honda Civic. I had a lot of great memories in that car, but all I could think about was how terrible I felt on my sixteenth birthday.

That morning, my mother and father had some sort of legal fight. The argument was so bad, they forgot about my birthday until later that night.

Two days later, I had to take Amos, my golden retriever, to the vet to be put to sleep, as he was painfully dying from cancer. I'd had him since I was ten years old. He loved to hike, swim, and play. When my parents were going through their divorce, Amos was always by my side. He slept by my bed from the night he showed up at my doorstep until the morning we put him to sleep. He was my best friend. And I took him to die.

I didn't think life could get any worse. I was wrong.

The next week, as I was driving to visit my brother at college, my friend David's mom passed me, her sister and niece in the car with her. I waved, then moments later pulled over to get gas. Twenty-five minutes after I got back on my way, I saw that a car had gone off the road into a ditch. I considered pulling over to see if I could help, but the car didn't seem to be in very bad shape. I figured everybody was OK, and I might cause an accident myself if I stopped, so I continued on to Mel's dorm.

I was hanging out in my brother's room with some of his friends when my cell phone rang. My father told me David's mom had been killed in a car accident about an hour ago.

I was consumed with guilt. If I had pulled over, maybe I could have saved her life. This woman left behind five children between the ages of eight and twenty. My heart broke for the entire family, especially my best friend David.

In shock and disbelief, I called David and told him I loved him and that I would always be there for him. But that didn't assuage my guilt.

That night I drank until I passed out.

I continued to lose all faith in God. How could He let my parents divorce? How could He let my church split? How could He allow my dog and David's mom to die? If God was so good, why was everything around me so bad?

Now I realize that life, even the Christian life, was never created to be easy. All human beings go through hard times. The difference between those who know and love the Lord versus those who don't is that when we go through tough times, the Lord is there to give us peace. We know He will carry us through them.

For the next two years I put on a front to my family, my school, and my church. I pretended I was fine so everyone would leave me alone. But I wanted out of this life.

During my senior year of high school, I transferred to a school that only required me to attend Monday through Wednesday. Every Wednesday night I drove five hours to Mammoth, where I skied and stayed with my new girlfriend Lauren. I left on Sunday morning in time to get back for church.

As the season progressed, my skills improved. I competed in major competitions. Just two years before, I was watching ski movies and ESPN competitions with the best skiers in the world. Now here I was, not only competing against my idols, but placing next to them in competition.

In June 2003 I graduated from high school, which was quite an accomplishment since school was a constant struggle and sports was all I cared about. I spent the summer after graduation working as a lifeguard at a local pool, and in August I decided to move to Mammoth to pursue skiing full time and to be with my girlfriend.

I was still upset at what had happened in my life, but I knew in my heart there had to be some sort of Creator, I just had no interest in getting to know this God. Obviously He didn't care about me.

When I told my dad I was moving to Mammoth, he asked why. I gave him the answer he wanted to hear by saying I believed God wanted me to. He asked why I thought that. I told him I felt I could be a good witness to the athletes I came in contact with. He gave me a suspicious look, but didn't argue.

As I thought about what I said to my father, I started to convince myself that I really was being sent by God. Perhaps I would find Him in my pursuit of being a skier. Within a few days I was convinced that it must be the Lord's will.

A week later I headed out to Mammoth. Within a few months I became a stupid, drunken, fornicating jerk, which finally led to my demise.

Σ QTA Ɜ

Chapter 9
Changed

In February 2004, after six years of living in debauchery, I found myself beginning to search out God. I knew the Lord had brought me home. But I still didn't understand why. All I did know was that I was responsible for my relationship with God. I wasn't going to do something simply because others were doing it, or because someone suggested it. My relationship with the Lord was between Him and me.

As I began to seek out God, I also sought out new relationships. I started dating Aimee, the girl I'd known since fourth grade whose name had appeared on my cell phone when I was at Stanford Hospital getting checked out after my concussion. I'd called and left her a message, but returned to Mammoth before she could return my call. Fortunately, when I moved home, I ran into her at the store where she reminded me we needed to catch up on an unfinished phone call. I contacted her again and we started hanging out together.

Aimee loved the Lord and had the same goals and desires I did. She was still a believer, but was struggling with the Christian lifestyle. Like me, she'd been hurt in previous relationships and was searching for purpose.

I wanted to ask her out but was hesitant about dating. I'd just come out of a crazy relationship. I'd never dated a Christian. But I wanted to see how a relationship would work when God was in the middle of it. Within a few weeks, it was easy to tell we were falling for each other. One night while we were parked downtown in my little Volkswagen convertible, we decided to take a chance and started dating.

In the Spring of 2004, I re-enrolled in college, got my old job as a lifeguard and went to church every Sunday.

My life appeared to be on track. But within a few months, I began to doubt if the Lord had really brought me home. I still didn't know what I was supposed to do with my life. Should I pursue skiing when my health returned? Or should I stay in my hometown and finish college? What career should I go into? Would I marry Aimee?

I shared some of my questions with Aimee. She gave me solid, wise answers. But there were secrets of my heart such as marriage, faith and my personal struggles with pornography and sexual desires which I could not share with anyone. Only God knew them and only God could answer them and help me.

In the meantime, I stuck with the choices I'd made. I determined to stay with my girlfriend, keep going to school, and continue reading the Bible and attending church regularly.

I studied Criminal Justice with a general concentration in Criminal Law. I looked into areas of law-enforcement work, such as probation officer, police officer, DA investigator, game warden, and lawyer by reading about and interviewing people in each profession.

After taking a tour of a police station in Santa Cruz CA, I was hooked. I figured I could work my way up from street cop to investigator, make good money, and provide for a family. But that station was a couple of hours away from my home, and the local law enforcement agencies were small and I wanted the action the larger city police departments offered. Working there would mean moving and finding a new church. Still, I wondered if it might be the Lord's will for me to pursue a career there.

Remembering the last time I thought I knew the Lord's will, I felt torn. I'd honestly believed He wanted me to go to Mammoth, but that's where I lost everything. My conscience wouldn't let me do or plan anything.

I contemplated quitting school, moving back to Mammoth, and returning to skiing. But I didn't want to make any rash decisions. A few years earlier I would have done whatever my feelings told me to do. Now I was certain that God had a plan for my life, and I was afraid I would never be complete if I stepped out of His plan.

Scared and uncertain about my future I drove home from the tour of the police station, when a friend from church called and invited me to a get-together at his house to study the Bible. I went to Mike's place, expecting to hang out with a few guys, talk about our days, and perhaps do a little Bible study. Little did I know, my life was about to change forever.

For the first fifteen minutes, we talked about prayer, showing the love of Christ to others, and trying to live good lives. Then Mike brought up the topic of "manifesting the presence of God."

I asked him what he meant by that expression. He said,

"Have you ever been in church, worshipping God, and then you felt a strong presence in the room?"

I told him about the time I went to the chapel at church camp and felt so awestruck I couldn't walk straight.

"That was the presence of the Lord."

Mike said, "When we truly love God, He dwells within us everywhere, all the time." He used Scripture to prove his point.

"But how do we manifest the presence of the Lord?" I asked.

He compared it to a flower that drops seeds, which then become flowers of the same species. Jesus chose us, and we are to become just like Him, imitating His very life.

Everything in me wanted to live a life that reflected Jesus' character. He was wise, loving, and kind, but He was also a strong man who lived what He believed, not compromising, even to the point of his own death. I wanted to live this way, but how? I figured I had a long way to go before I could manifest the presence of the Lord in my life.

While other people in the group voiced opinions and read from Scripture. While they were talking, I felt an intense heat on the right side of my body, from the top of my head to the bottoms of my feet. Out of the corner of my eye, I saw Mike with his arms stretched out and his hands open toward me. When I faced him, he dropped his arms and acted like he hadn't done anything unusual.

I thought, what a weirdo.

A minute or so later, my entire body became hot, as if a warm robe had been thrown over it. I again saw Mike with his arms stretched out toward me and hands wide open. This time, when I looked his way, he did not drop his arms. As they remained up and outstretched, I felt God's love and presence surround me.

I made eye contact with Mike, and his arms lowered.

"Anaiah," he said, "God's very presence is here, and in His presence is love."

"He wants you to know He is with you, He loves you and will never let you go. You are His, bought by His blood."

My soul broke. I buried my head between my legs, fighting tears. Suddenly there was complete silence in the room, and I heard a voice say, "Be still and know that I am God."

Overwhelmed by God's presence, I silently screamed out to God, *I'm tired of compromising. And I'm tired of having doubts about You and Your plans for my life. I'm sick of worrying about my future and what career to go into. I want to forgive the people who have hurt me. I don't want to play these stupid games. I want a relationship with You. I want whatever You have for me. I want Your will. I want Your presence in my life. Please don't leave me, change me or let me go!*

A man from the group put his hand on my shoulder. "Anaiah, I don't know what's going through your mind right now, but the Lord is here. He wants to heal your broken heart and show You His love. If you give yourself to Him, you won't have to worry about your future, about what job you'll have. You will be able to show love and forgiveness, even to those who may not deserve it, because God has shown you love and forgiveness. Just be still and let God work in your heart."

Hearing him say out loud the words that had been going through my head amazed me. I was overcome by the presence of the Lord.

As I sat there, I recalled the preacher who said there would someday be people who would do greater things than Jesus did. I realized he'd been referring to John 14:12, which says, "Verily, verily, I say unto you, He that believeth on me, the works that I do shall he do also; and greater works than these shall he do; because I go unto my Father," and Matthew 5:4–5, which says, "Be perfect just as your father in heaven is perfect" (KJV).

The presence of the Lord was so heavy on me, I collapsed face down on the floor. As I lay there, I handed every part of my life over to God. My goals, my dreams, my aspirations. My past, my present, my future. I told God that everything I had was His.

The moment I said these words, I experienced something that is almost impossible to describe. As I lay on the floor with my eyes closed I saw what appeared to be flashes of light. It was like looking into a strobe light. As I looked into the light, each flash brought back a memory of God which began to restore my faith in Him.

One flash was a memory of me laying on the church floor at the age of 2. Another was a memory of me worshipping God in Jr. church; another flash jolted a memory of learning about king David's tabernacle in the wilderness.

With each flash came a restoration of my faith, mind and heart. It was like God was cleaning out the viruses that plagued my life and then downloading a better, restored system.

After about an hour, I tried to stand up, but I was so weak I had to sit down. As I sat, I realized I had just met with God and was never going to be the same. I was changed. For the first time in my life God was no longer a mythical idea, but a real, loving being.

Σ **QTA** Ƹ

Chapter 10
Fighting for It

The Bible study came to an end around midnight. Instead of heading home, I drove to my girlfriend's house to tell her what had happened. But as I was driving, my mind—which moments ago was filled with joy, peace, and purpose—became full of doubt and confusion. I began to wonder if my amazing encounter with God had been real or just an emotional high.

Then I heard the Lord say, "Pick up your sword."

I knew Satan was the one causing me to doubt, and God wanted me to take up the only spiritual weapon I had at my disposal and use it.

I screamed out loud, "No way, Satan! You will not take my joy. You will not take my peace. You will not take my purpose. Get away from me. Your reign here is over. No longer are your plans going to succeed in my life." I asked God to take the doubts that were flooding my mind far from me.

Right there in the car, the presence of the Lord fell even stronger than it did at Mike's house.

When I arrived at Aimee's place, she was asleep, so I

called her on my cell phone.

"I'm outside your house, and I have to talk to you."

"What's wrong?" Her voice sounded scared.

"Just come outside."

Moments later she opened the door, a puzzled expression on her face. "You look different." She told me my face seemed to be lit up.

I tried to explain to her what had happened, but all I could get out of my mouth was "God loves me so much and called me to manifest the life of Jesus. God is calling me to Him and wants so badly for me to know Him like Jesus knew Him while He walked this earth. He's calling me to live holy before Him."

Her mouth dropped open.

I told her I felt like Moses as he stood before the burning bush. She said my face looked like I'd just had a burning-bush experience.

I went to bed that night exhausted. When I woke up the next morning, I had an intense desire to read the Bible. I felt physically hungry for the Word.

After reading Scripture for about a half hour, I got in the shower and sang worship songs in my head. Again, doubts crept into my mind. Was what happened last night real? I knew right away what was going on.

"Satan, I told you last night to leave me alone. The blood of Jesus is over me. You have no place here." Immediately I felt my doubts break.

I then realized that I'd have a spiritual target on my back for the rest of my life. Every day, Satan would be waiting for an opportunity to shake and even break my faith. If I was going to hold on to God's promises, I needed to fight.

I recalled 1 Peter 5:8–9: "Be self-controlled and alert. Your enemy the devil prowls around like a roaring lion looking for someone to devour. Resist him, standing firm in the faith, because you know that your brothers throughout the world are undergoing the same kind of sufferings."

"Be self-controlled and alert," "resist him, standing firm in the faith," I said over and over while standing in the shower. Then I made it personal. "Anaiah," I said to myself, "grow up and stop acting immature. Be self-controlled in everything you do and every decision you make. Stay alert. When you see situations that test your faith, resist the devil and stand firm in your faith."

Σ **QTA** Ƹ

Chapter 11
Equipped

As I continued to read the Bible, pray and talk to God daily, He showed me that I needed to get water baptized in order to strengthen my life and walk with Him.

Excited about my life-changing encounter with God, and eager to dive into everything the Lord had to offer, I visited my pastor and asked if I could participate in the water baptism that was to take place the following week. He had heard about what happened to me a few weeks earlier and was excited that I was interested. But he cautioned, "Water baptism is not a small thing."

"I know, Pastor, and I'm not taking it lightly."

"Then do you mind if I ask you some personal questions?"

"Go ahead."

"Are you sleeping with your girlfriend?"

His question caught me off guard. Fortunately, Aimee and I had recently decided to stop having sex, so I could honestly reply, "No, not anymore."

"Do you have any problems with pornography?"

I felt uncomfortable talking about this stuff with him. "Off and on."

He switched direction and asked me why I wanted to be baptized.

I was prepared for that question. "I want a new heart, a fresh start, a clean slate. I want to get rid of my sins and bury the old man that I was. I want to take on the family name of God, the Lord Jesus Christ. I want to rise to a new life and a new way of living."

I expected to hear, "Wow, Anaiah, it sounds like you're ready to get baptized. I'll put you on the list for next week." Instead my pastor quoted me Luke 3:8: "Produce fruit in keeping with repentance." He explained that I needed to show proof that I had repented from unclean acts and attitudes.

I went home that day and did some research in the Bible, and sure enough, he was right.

The following Sunday, my pastor preached an awesome message about water baptism and then baptized around a dozen people. Most of them were teens or young adults I'd known for years. I was excited for them . . . but also envious.

I enrolled in a six-month baptism class with my girlfriend. I wasn't particularly thrilled about taking it. I preferred dissecting the Word at home alone in my room. I believed the Holy Spirit was a better teacher than any human being. But for six months I showed up.

During those six months I kept track of the young people who'd been baptized the week I'd wanted to. I expected them to do awesome things for the church and for the Lord. Instead I saw several of them backsliding. Some got caught up in drinking, having sex, and rebelling. These kids seemed worse off now than before they were baptized.

I wondered if water baptism was real after all. When I asked the Lord about this, He led me to Matthew 3:16–4:11:

> As soon as Jesus was baptized, he went up out of the water. At that moment heaven was opened, and he saw the Spirit of God descending like a dove and landed on him. And a voice from heaven said, "This is my Son, whom I love; with him I am well pleased."
>
> Then Jesus was led by the Spirit into the desert to be tempted by the devil. After fasting forty days and forty nights, he was hungry. The tempter came to him and said, "If you are the Son of God, tell these stones to become bread."
>
> Jesus answered, "It is written: 'Man does not live on bread alone, but on every word that comes from the mouth of God.'"
>
> Then the devil took him to the holy city and had him stand on the highest point of the temple. "If you are the Son of God," he said, "throw yourself down. For it is written: 'He will command his angels concerning you, and they will lift you up in their hands, so that you will not strike your foot against a stone.'"
>
> Jesus answered him, "It is also written: 'Do not put the Lord your God to the test.'"
>
> Again, the devil took him to a very high mountain and showed him all the kingdoms of the world and their splendor. "All this I will give you," he said, "if you will bow down and worship me."
>
> Jesus said to him, "Away from me, Satan! For it is written: 'Worship the Lord your God, and serve him only.'"

Then the devil left him, and angels came and attended him.

After Jesus was baptized He did not have an easy day; He was immediately tempted. He had fasted forty days and was hungry. I feel weak if I don't eat every four or five hours. Imagine how vulnerable Jesus must have been after not eating for over a month. And there, at His weakest physical moment, Satan showed up. But Jesus used the Word of God to fight off the devil's temptations.

I'd wanted to get baptized so I could get rid of the unclean things I did and thought. I figured if I had a new spiritual heart and mind, I would be able to stop looking at pornography, stop craving sex, and live a better life. But after I read this passage in Matthew, I realized that baptism was not a quick fix to my problems, any more than accepting Christ as Savior means He takes away all our problems. The Christian walk is full of trials and tests of our faith.

The Lord showed me that those kids who'd been baptized wanted a new heart and mind, just like I had. But they didn't realize that they were placing a target on their back for Satan. So the devil had caught them off guard, and before they knew what hit them, they were entangled in sins.

Since many of these young people were friends of mine, I asked them why they got baptized. Their answers had a common theme. They'd all fallen into sins they wanted out of, and they figured baptism would give them a fresh start. They expected life to get easier afterward.

But water baptism had not taken away their problems. The urge to sin had not disappeared. No wonder Satan had so easily tricked them.

When I completed my six months of baptism class, the

pastor allowed me to be baptized. But as the date of my baptism grew closer, I became worried. I now understood what I was getting into. I hoped that knowledge would better prepare me to face the trials and temptations ahead of me.

By the time my baptismal Sunday arrived, I felt ready. I had not looked at one piece of pornographic material or had any form of sexual conduct with my girlfriend. I'd changed the way I dressed, spoke, and tithed my money. I'd changed the people I hung out with and the music I listened to.

I had determined in my heart to show the fruit of repentance to myself, God, and those around me.

I went under the baptismal water that day, just minutes after Aimee. When I came up out of the water, I sensed God's presence come down on me in a soft, gentle way. I knew the work had been done. Just as Ezekiel 36:26 stated, I now had a new heart and a new mind, able to write God's laws on my heart, but it was a choice I would have to make.

It would require getting to know my God on a daily basis in order for His ways to become relevant in my life.

Σ **QTA** Ƨ

Chapter 12
Trials

About eight months after I was baptized, the temptations I anticipated hit hard.

I left home to go to a California state university. Some of the classes I took tested my faith, and there were plenty of opportunities to party and cheat on the girl I knew the Lord had saved for me.

I wanted to complete two years of college in ten months, so I had a busy schedule. I attended classes from 7 a.m. till 9 or 10 at night, then studied as long as I could stay awake. I drove home on Wednesday nights to go to church, then headed back right after. I went home on Friday nights so I could volunteer on Saturdays at church work crews and hang out with Aimee. After church on Sunday I drove back to school.

I didn't think of being busy as a temptation. But how we use our time defines who we are. I knew I needed to schedule specific times to spend in the Word. But I didn't have any blocks of time to set aside. I felt disappointed that I couldn't spend hours in the Scriptures. But the Lord showed me in

Ephesians 6:13–18 that I could always be praying. We don't need to plan times with God; everything is His, at all times, in all places.

The Lord reminded me of the story of Adam and Eve in the book of Genesis. They lived in a beautiful garden where they dwelt with God, having a good time, enjoying each other's company. They weren't on a schedule.

It was liberating to know that I didn't need a set block of time to read my Bible. I could pray in the Spirit and worship the Lord anytime, anywhere: in the shower, while walking to class, in the middle of a boring lecture, while I was studying, when friends were begging me to go party, while sitting in a hot tub, when jogging. Whenever and wherever I wanted, I could praise Him!

A few weeks after this change took place in my outlook, people started noticing something different about me and asked me what it was. I realized it was the Lord's life manifesting out of me.

Almost every day I told someone my testimony about what the Lord had done for me and how excited I was.

After speaking to one person about the Lord, she said, "Anaiah, you have to write a book about all this."

"Everybody thinks they have a story to tell. That doesn't mean they should all write a book. Besides, I don't even like writing."

"But your story is something people can relate to. Maybe it could help an unbeliever find faith, a prodigal return to the Lord, or someone who's on the fence in their walk with God find balance and strength."

When I got home that night I thought about what that girl had said. Then I laughed out loud. How could I write a book? I barely passed English in high school, and I'd flunked the subject in grade school.

I continued telling my story to friends and strangers who seemed interested. Almost every Christian I talked to said I should write my story and put it in a book.

I began to seriously wonder if someone could be impacted by a book about my experiences. Would everything I had gone through and overcome be worth it if it benefited even one person?

The Lord showed me that my life was no longer mine but His.

I asked God if He wanted me to write my story. I did not get an immediate clear answer.

The next day I asked the same question. Still no answer.

I asked myself, Do you honestly think people could read your story and find purpose in their lives?

I truly believed that someone could be inspired to repent, change his ways, and get excited about starting a relationship with God by reading about what happened to me.

The Lord had given me a second chance. He'd healed areas of my heart that were so scarred I didn't even realize they were wounded. He restored relationships, gave me the ability to trust and love again. How could I not do something?

The next day, during my lunch break in the cafeteria, I said, OK, Lord, this book is going to be written . . . if for no other reason, so I can remind myself later in life what You've done for me and how great Your love is for me. If you want it for any other purpose, it's Yours.

I opened my laptop and began to write.

Σ **QTA** Ƹ

Chapter 13
Conclusion

I started writing this book in the Fall of 2005. I was twenty-one years old, in my senior year at college, and excited about my future. Now it's 2011. I am twenty-six years of age and happily married to Aimee, and we have a daughter. In that alone, I am blessed.

Looking back over the last six years or so, I have seen God's continued grace in my life. However, I have to admit, as I wrote the manuscript for this book, I wondered if the changes I'd experienced would be lifelong. I was afraid the spiritual high would eventually die down, leaving me where I was before. Part of the reason I waited so many years to publish this book was that I wanted to prove to myself the change was permanent.

I am here to tell you what I found to be the truth. Jesus Christ is Lord, He has changed my life for the better, and this truly is the life I always wanted.

Since asking the Lord into my heart, my life has not been peachy. It's full of ups and downs, happiness and sadness, moments of great confidence and moments of uncertainty.

However, I can't imagine living without the Creator. My fears of waking up one day and not wanting the Lord in my life have not come to pass. God has become such a reality to me, I will never be able to stay away from the pursuit of His presence.

I have continued to search out God in prayer and in His Word. The time I spent alone with God, sitting down with the Bible and searching Him out, has grounded and rooted my faith.

This book was written for those who may be in the shoes I was in before God changed my life. I want you to have the assurance I have. I am no superstar author, famous preacher, or Bible scholar with a doctorate degree. But I know one thing: God's love has changed my life. I want you to know there is hope. I want you to know God loves you and is waiting to meet with you.

The Bible says in Revelations 3:20, "I stand at the door and knock, if anyone hears my voice and opens the door, I will come into him and will dine with him and he with me."

Since the day you were born, God's knocking has been the heartbeat of your life. Daily he knocks giving you another chance to respond to Him. The tug that is on your heart and the unfulfilled areas in your life will never go away until you open the door to Jesus Christ.

Before I opened the door to Him, I was hungry for answers, peace, hope, fulfilment and purpose in this life. But when I opened my life to Jesus Christ, I found everything I had been looking for. It was just like Revelations 3:20 stated. Jesus came into my life and He dined with me, He fed my soul and provided the nourishment my life was lacking.

If you and your family were extremely poor and you

found ten million dollars, would you not take that money and give it to all your loved ones? Would you not want a better life for you and for them? Well, I found something far better than money, and I want you to have it. Will you consider accepting it?

If so, I want you to read the prayer that changed my life seven years ago and consider praying it yourself. If you do so in sincerity, I promise you He will not let you down.

> *"Lord, I'm tired of compromising and I'm tired of having doubts about you and your plans for my life. I'm sick of worrying about my future and what will become of me. I want to forgive the people who have hurt me and be able to love and trust again. I don't want to play stupid games; back and forth with You. I want a relationship. I want whatever you have for me. I want your will and presence in my life. Thank you for dying on the cross for me. Today, I accept the fact that You are my God, that you love me and that I am yours. I will commit to getting to know You better and I know that you're going to make yourself a reality to me. Amen"*

This book was simply a memoir of the events which lead up to my life changing encounter with God. However since 2005, I have continued to search out God in prayer and in his word. It was the time spent alone with God, sitting down with his word and searching Him out which has really grounded and rooted my faith.

During this time, I became aware of how the routine, everyday life affected me. The music I listened to, alcohol and the friends I hung out with were areas in my life that the Lord showed me needed change. In particular, like most men I struggled with an addiction to pornography, sex and a mind that could never seem to forget.

As the Lord began to convict me of the changes needed in my life, I searched out God for His answers and help. Throughout my journey, I documented the struggles I faced and compiled them into a book of helpful guidelines on how to over come through Christ. It was during this time, I found out who I was in Christ and the power I had through that understanding. In the end, I found myself changed and victorious in every area of my life.

If you share the same struggles I faced, then I would encourage you to read my next book. It reveals how God views your struggles and how to align your life with His in order to carry out His will in your life. Finally, it will empower you to walk with God in purity.

Visit: http://www.TheLifeIAlwaysWanted.com
for details on my next book.

Σ **Questions To Think About** Ƨ

As promised in the Introduction, here are some questions for you to think about as you read this book. Jot down your answers here or in a journal or notebook.

Chapter 3

What is the worst thing that has ever happened to you?

How did you respond to the hurt you went through (for example, taking drugs, drinking alcohol, becoming unsocial, cutting classes, praying, counseling)?

Chapter 4a

Have you ever been in a situation so bad that you wondered if there was a God? If so, did He answer? How did He answer (through His Word, through another person, through songs or dreams)? What did He say to you?

In order to hear from God, you must allow Him to talk to you. One way you can do this is by opening the Bible and asking God to talk to you through His Word. If you've never done this before, I encourage you to try it.

Chapter 4b

Has God ever answered a prayer of yours in a dramatic way?

Was the answer you received what you wanted to hear?

Did you initially reject what the Lord showed you, or did you immediately accept it?

What actions did you perform that showed you had chosen to accept what God showed you? (My example was packing my stuff and going back home.)

Chapter 4c

Do you think I was crazy to talk out loud to God? (It's okay if you say yes. I thought I was a little crazy myself.) Have you ever tried it? If so, what happened?

Does it seem like coincidence that after all those horrible things happened to me, the Bible, my aunt, and a preacher spoke directly to my situation? Or do you think God was trying to get my attention?

If you were in my situation, would you have decided to go home? Why or why not?

Do you have some doubts about God? Or do you know without a doubt that He is real and that He allows things to happen to us in order to get our attention?

Chapter 5

Have you ever experienced the reality of heaven or hell? If so, what was it like? Did it open your eyes to the fact that there is a God and a devil?

If you've never had an encounter with heaven or hell, consider asking God to show you the reality of the spiritual world. I'm not encouraging you to seek out demonic forces. But if you ask God to open your eyes to the spiritual world, as I did, what you experience may cause you to seek after God more passionately.

Chapter 6

Have you ever had an experience where you felt the presence of God?

If you haven't, would you be open to searching out God's presence? If not, why not? What is holding you back?

Chapter 7

Have you ever gone through something that you felt stole part of your soul, your trust, a relationship, or even your beliefs? Think about what happened and what you lost.

What did you replace this loss with? (For me, my outlet was skiing.)

Chapter 8

Have you ever hit rock bottom? What happened?

How did you deal with your situation? (I moved to Mammoth.)

If you would have been patient and waited instead of striking out on your own, do you think your circumstances would have been different? Why?

Chapter 9

Have you ever had a miraculous experience with God that you knew was real?

Was all the doubt in your heart completely removed by that experience?

If you have had one of those life-changing appointments with God, write down every detail you remember of exactly what happened. It may take up a single page, or it might turn into a book. Put your written account somewhere that you know you will never lose it. Get it out every couple years to remind yourself what God did for you and how He made Himself real to you.

If you've never had a life-changing experience with God, do you wish you could? If so, ask Him to reveal Himself to you. Sometimes He shows Himself in little ways. Occasionally He does something absolutely amazing.

If you're serious about meeting with God in a way

that will completely change your life, write down all the things you need to surrender: control, relationships, work, education, etc. If you are unsure, ask God to show you. Then make that decision to surrender, based not on emotions but on your relationship with the Lord. If you ask God to completely change your life, be ready—He will!

Chapter 10

Have you ever doubted a miraculous work that God did in your life, even immediately after it took place?

What did you do to overcome that doubt?

What should you do?

Research and write down Scriptures that deal with spiritual warfare. Start with Ephesians 6:13–18 and 2 Corinthians 10:5.

How would you train for spiritual warfare if you knew your enemy wanted to destroy your life?

Chapter 11

Have you experienced water baptism? If so, did you notice a change in your life afterward?

Did you notice temptations after water baptism?

If you have never been baptized, why not? What are you waiting for?

Chapter 12

Has the Lord given you a second chance? Has He healed areas of your heart that were so scarred you didn't even realize they were wounded? Has He restored relationships, given you the ability to trust and love again? Do you feel compelled to do something for God in return?

Have you ever wondered if the story of your life might be beneficial to someone else? Do you think people could read your story and find purpose in their lives? Might someone be inspired to repent, change his ways, and get excited about starting a relationship with God by reading about what happened to you?

Perhaps you've thought about writing your story but don't know how to begin. Or maybe you started writing once or twice, but gave up. If nothing else, write your story so you can remind yourself later what God has done for you and how great His love is for you. Then pray about what He would have you do with it.

If you feel led to share your story with others, even your own family and friends, seek out a professional author or editor to help you get it in shape and get it into print. If you haven't done that yet, what's stopping you?

> *"They overcame by the blood of the lamb and the word of their testimony."*
>
> ~ Revelations 12:11

ABOUT THE AUTHOR

Anaiah Kirk is 26 years old and lives near Yosemite in California with his wife Aimee and their daughter Amelia. After graduating from California State University Stanislaus in 2006 with a Bachelor's degree in Criminal Justice, he became  a Juvenile Probation Officer where he then transferred to the Department of Corrections and now works as a Correctional Counselor.

Anaiah loves the outdoors. He has climbed several mountains including Mt. Langley, Mt. Muir, Mt. Whitney, Mt. Shasta and Mt. Dana and has hiked the famous "John Muir Trail" stretching 220 miles. He has been involved with youth ministry since the age of 19 by teaching at church, summer church camps and on backpacking retreats. His hearts desire is to see his generation find a personal relationship with Christ and live a pure and moral life in this world.

Visit him at www.TheLifeIAlwaysWanted.com

www.ingramcontent.com/pod-product-compliance
Lightning Source LLC
Chambersburg PA
CBHW060846050426
42453CB00008B/847